NEW ZEALAND

MOUNTAINS TO THE SEA

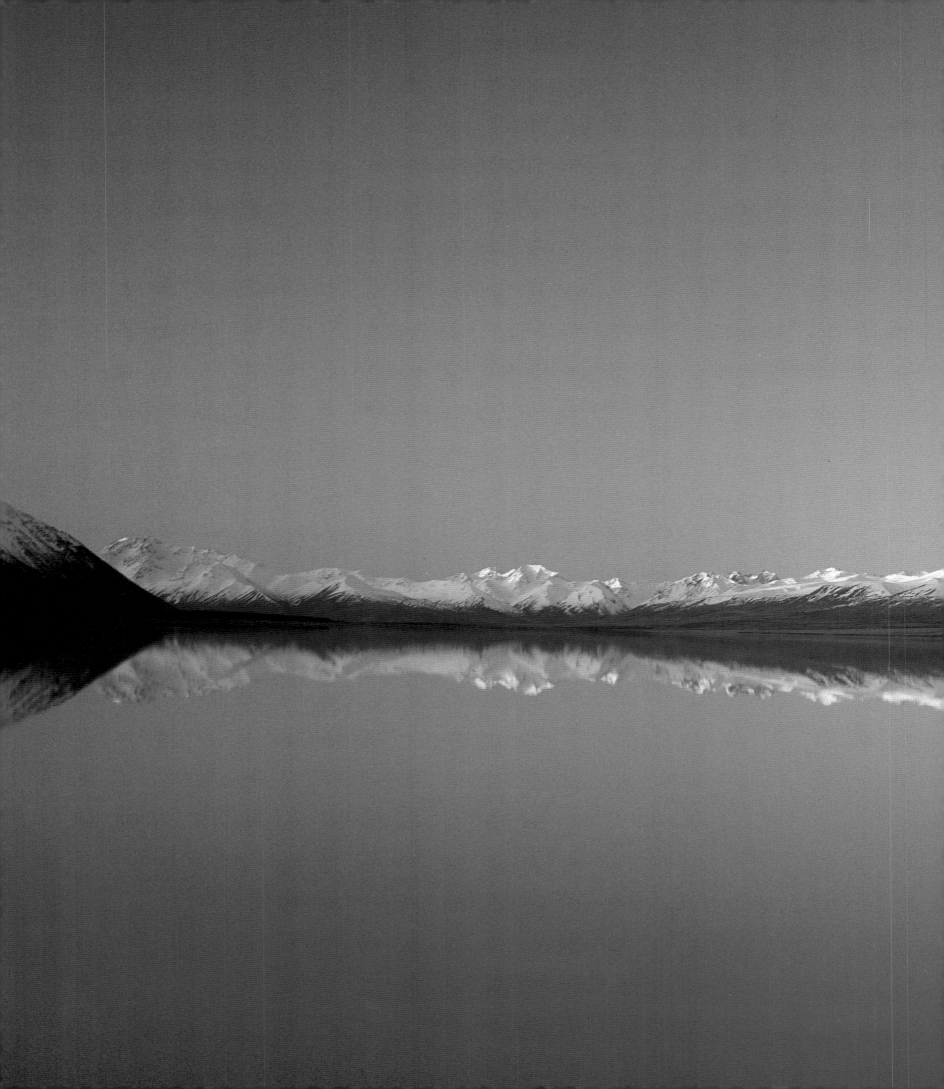

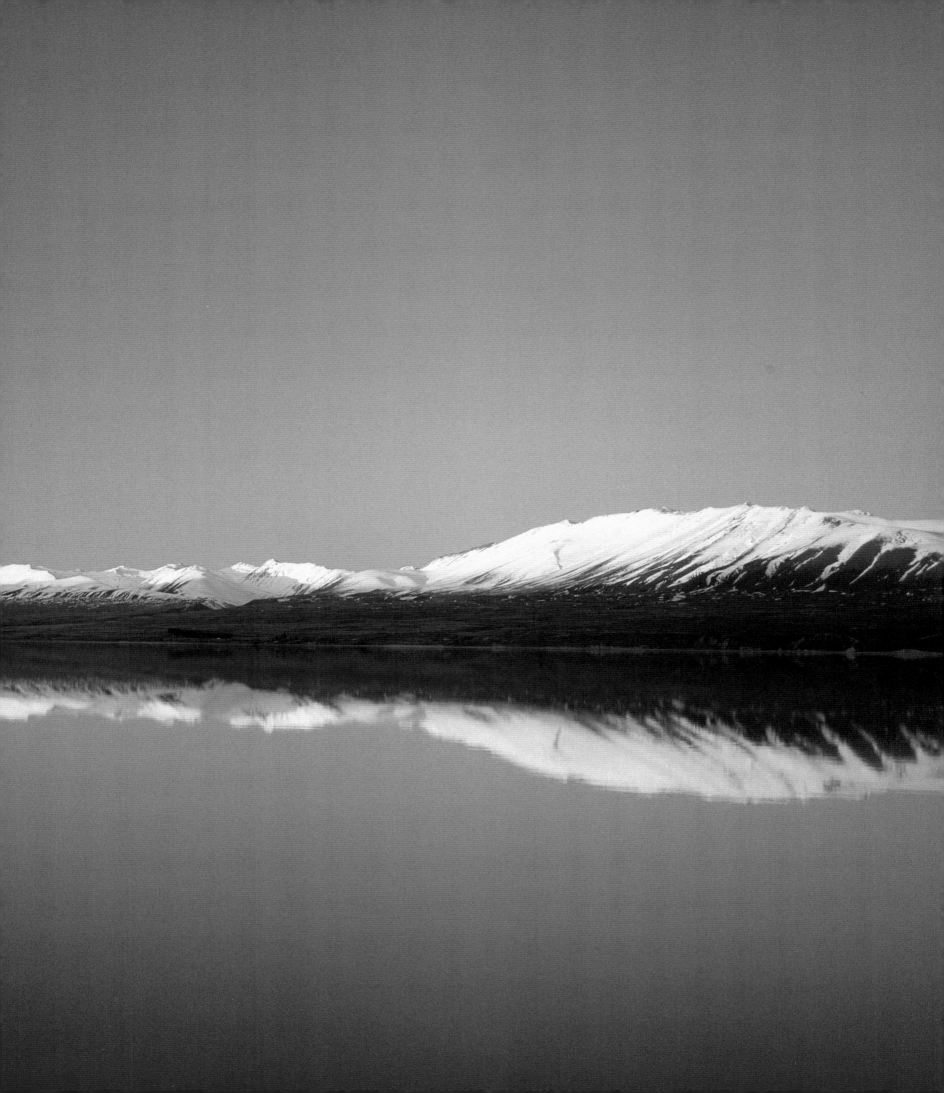

Lion Peak, Milford Sound

NEW ZEALAND

MOUNTAINS TO THE SEA

photographs by

WARREN JACOBS

text by

JOHN WILSON

KOWHAI
PUBLISHING

CONTENTS

Published by Kowhai Publishing Ltd
R.D. 1 Lyttelton and
10 Peacock Street, Auckland

First published 1994

ISBN 0–908598–59–9

Design by John Burt and Warren Jacobs
Finished artwork by John Burt Graphics, Christchurch
Set in Friz Quadrata, Garamond Book Italic and
Copperplate Gothic by Type Shop Ltd, Christchurch
Film positives made in Hong Kong
Printed in Hong Kong

Endpaper:
Morning Mist, Hagley Park, Christchurch
Pages 2–3: Lake Tekapo & Southern Alps
Pages 4–5: Kenepuru Sound, Marlborough Sounds
Page 8:   Fox Glacier, South Westland

Department of Survey and Land Information
Map Licence No. PL 098425/1

10

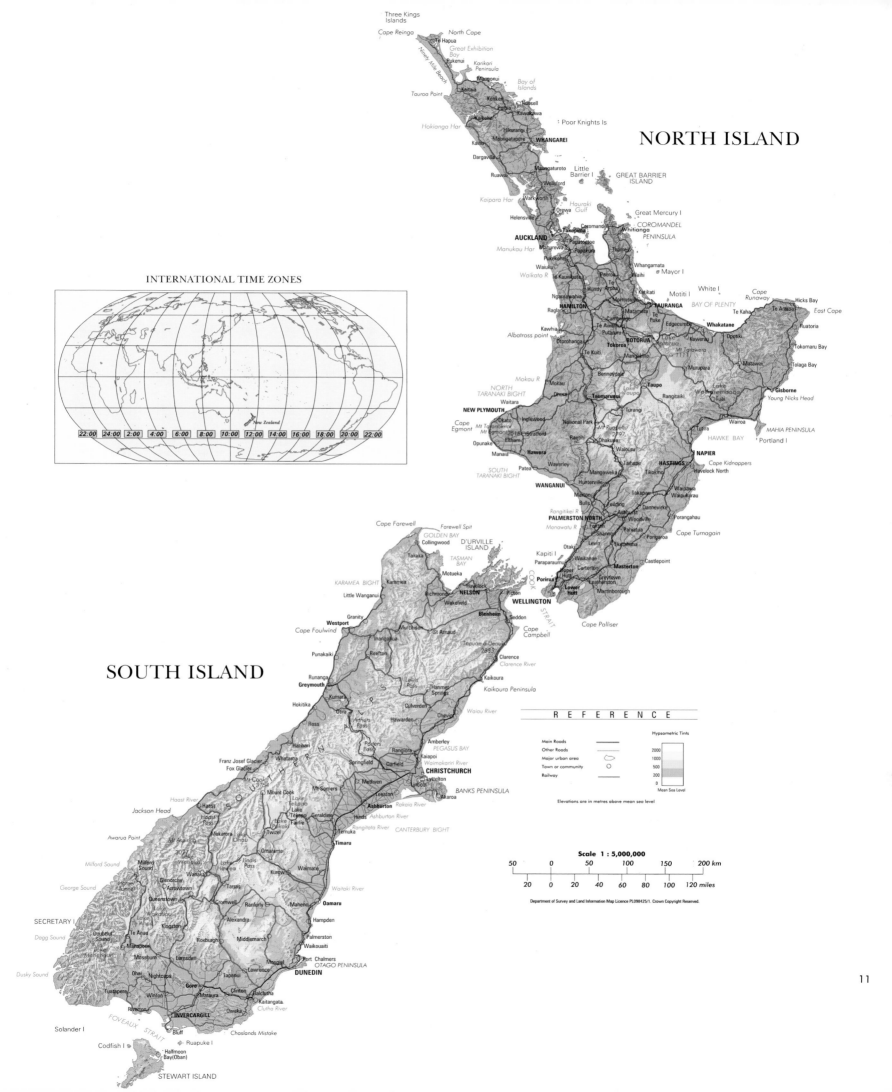

NORTH ISLAND

SOUTH ISLAND

INTERNATIONAL TIME ZONES

22:00 24:00 2:00 4:00 6:00 8:00 10:00 12:00 14:00 16:00 18:00 20:00 22:00

New Zealand

REFERENCE

Main Roads
Other Roads
Major urban area
Town or community
Railway

Hypsometric Tints
2000
1000
500
200
0
Mean Sea Level

Elevations are in metres above mean sea level

Scale 1 : 5,000,000

50   0   50   100   150   200 km
20   0   20   40   60   80   100   120 miles

Department of Survey and Land Information Map Licence PL098425/1. Crown Copyright Reserved.

11

INTRODUCTION

In my New Zealand childhood, ignorant of the rest of the world, I was proud and quietly satisfied when told that New Zealand had, in its landscapes, a little of the best of all other countries. I grew up believing that our sounds were more than a match for Norway's fiords, our mountains for Switzerland's alps; that we had settled countryside as beautiful as any part of rural England; that our plains were as open and dramatic as those of the American Mid West. What other country had both thermal regions and glaciers? (Several, I discovered later!) All New Zealand lacked, we conceded grudgingly (as we had to, with Australia our only near neighbour) were proper deserts, though we were almost convinced that the arid lands of Central Otago and parts of the North Island's desolate volcanic plateau were as good as real deserts.

Later I was forced to acknowledge that perhaps there were mountain ranges grander than New Zealand's, coastlines more magnificent, forests more verdant. But my youthful complacency about the landscapes of my native land was not entirely unjustified. New Zealand has greater variety in its landscapes than almost any other country and, perhaps more importantly, quite different landscapes and environments are remarkably close together and easily accessible from the country's largest cities. From my home city of Christchurch, swimming and boating in the sheltered bays and harbours of Banks Peninsula are an hour's drive away; hiking, skiing or climbing in magnificent mountain lands are almost as close. I can leave the city in the morning and by lunchtime be walking in native forest as beautiful and profoundly peaceful as the forest being enjoyed by a tramper on Fiordland's Kepler Track (opposite). Aucklanders are perhaps not quite so fortunately situated, but their warm northern beaches are only two or three hours' drive from the alpine landscapes of the volcanoes of the central North Island.

There are geographical reasons for the diversity of New Zealand's landscapes in a relatively small land area. New Zealand is a long, skinny country, with two large and many smaller islands in a mid-ocean setting. The islands sit on one of the most geologically active places on the earth's surface, athwart the line of contact of two geological plates. From north to south, New Zealand stretches from about eleven degrees below the Tropic of Capricorn to about twenty degrees north of the Antarctic Circle. The country ranges from the nearly sub-tropical north to the next to sub-antarctic south. Further, mountain ranges have been thrust up in the path of prevailing westerly winds, resulting in high precipitation to the west and areas of 'rain shadow' to the east. It is often only a short distance from dense rain forest to semi-arid tussock grasslands.

New Zealand may not be quite the unique country I believed it to be in my childhood; but it is a special place, of great variety and beauty. Discover these islands with us . . .

T H E   C O A S T S

Bays, beaches, harbours, headlands & sounds

In the far north of New Zealand, Cape Reinga (left), beckons towards the tropical islands further north from which New Zealand's first inhabitants, the Maori, came on great canoes more than a thousand years ago. To this day, Cape Reinga is sacred to the Maori as the point from which the spirits of the dead depart for the underworld, one of their last sights the bright red of the pohutukawa which clings to the cliff side, wonderfully evocative of the spirits' reluctance to leave the world of light.

Perhaps nothing better illustrates the great variety of New Zealand's scenery and landscapes than its long coastline. For 1,600 kilometres south of Cape Reinga, the tough scrub on Stewart Island's rock-bound South Cape is sculpted by fierce southerly winds that blow unimpeded from Antarctica.

In general, the west coasts of both of New Zealand's main islands are wilder than those of the east, but there are sheltered harbours to the west and wild open beaches of sand and gravel to the east (both island's have a Ninety Mile Beach, the north's on the west coast, the south's on the east). Other open coasts are rocky, and dramatic headlands and capes jut out into sometimes wild seas. But there are also myriad sheltered harbours and bays; in some, native bush still reaches down to the sea, the blue sea separated from the green bush by a strand of golden or white sand. New Zealanders frequent their varied coasts at all times of the year — to swim, to boat, to walk on coastal walkways, to gather seafood from waters that are still unpolluted (at least away from centres of population). Life without easy access to the sea is unimaginable for most who live in New Zealand.

The shores of the peninsula of Northland, which projects from the isthmus occupied by New Zealands largest city, Auckland, illustrate the variety of the countrys coastline. To the west, surf from the Tasman Sea thunders onto long beaches. At the top end of Ninety Mile Beach, near Cape Reinga, a wild and remote Cape Maria van Diemen (this page, top) bears a name given by the first European navigator known to have visited New Zealand waters, the Dutchman Abel Tasman. But on the east coast of Northland are the sheltered havens of such harbours as Whangaroa (right) and the Bay of Islands. A feature of many of Northlands lovely bays, like Matai Bay (this page, above) between Rangaunu and Doubtless Bays, is the spectacular crimson blossom of the New Zealand Christmas tree, pohutukawa.

Warm waters, long summer days and sheltered harbours and bays draw week-end sailors and holidaymakers in large numbers to Northland. Many bays have clusters of 'baches' or holiday homes, which in the past were usually simple, even crude structures but are now often more commodious. Just off-shore, launches and yachts find safe anchorage, as at Tutukaka (left) east of Northland's main city, Whangarei. But even in the frequented waters of Northland it is still possible to find deserted coves where gnarled pohutukawa stand sentinel above rocky shorelines, as at Otamure Bay (above).

The Bay of Islands is the historic cradle of modern New Zealand, and a mecca of boaties from throughout the country. The evidence of this is the number of boats moored in Matauwhi Bay and off Russell (above) and also off Tapeka, near Russell, (opposite page). Russell is New Zealands oldest European town, and buildings remain from the days when rowdy Kororareka (Russells original name) was a major port of call for vessels whaling in the Pacific. But pleasure craft now ride at anchor on Bay of Islands waters where whaling ships once moored. One of the islands which prompted Captain Cook, the British navigator who placed New Zealand firmly on the map of the world, to give the bay its name is Urupukapuka (right).

East of Auckland is another peninsula, smaller than that of Northland, but more mountainous. The Coromandel Peninsula also has a wealth of bays, harbours and spectacular seascapes. At the tip of the Peninsula, Port Jackson (preceding page) looks across the Hauraki Gulf to populous Auckland, many of the residents of which look to the Coromandel for recreation and pleasure.

Restless seas have carved much of New Zealand's rocky shoreline into magnificent cliffs, headlands, sea stacks and islets, like those on the coast near Hahei (left), on the Coromandel, or at Piha, west of Auckland where Lion Rock (this page, top) thrusts its bold form out of the surf. Elsewhere, coastal rocks have been worn down to gentler level sea platforms or low reefs, as at Kuaotunu (above) north of Whitianga, many still prolific with delicacies such as mussels, paua (New Zealand abalone) and crayfish.

From the high forested hills around it, the Coromandel Harbour (above), from which the Peninsula took its name, still looks much as New Zealand must have appeared to the first people who came to its shores more than a thousand years ago. But there is a small settlement on the Coromandel Harbour itself, and on the eastern side of the Peninsula, Tokaroa Point and Pauanui (right), where many Aucklanders have holiday or retirement homes, it is clearly evident that parts of the New Zealand coast are subject to development pressures.

From Koputauaki Bay (left, opposite page) on the Coromandel Peninsula, the view is west across the Hauraki Gulf. There is nothing to suggest, as the day dies in a brilliant sunset, that New Zealand's most populous city is just over the horizon.

Between the Coromandel Peninsula and the East Cape lies the broad sweep of what Captain Cook called the Bay of Plenty, because he was able to replenish water and supplies with ease on its shores. At the Bay of Plenty's eastern extreme, Hicks Bay (above) epitomises the solitude that is still easy to find on New Zealand beaches.

The Maketu Estuary (left, this page) was one of the landfalls, and the last resting place, of the Arawa canoe. From those who voyaged on the Arawa to New Zealand sprang the powerful confederation of Maori tribes that occupy the inland Bay of Plenty.

Maori and Pakeha traditions and history blend at Anaura Bay (above) where Captain Cook anchored in October 1769, less than two weeks after first sighting New Zealand, and was received in friendly fashion by the resident Maori.

Lottin Point (left, opposite page) is one of the many fine headlands that punctuate the coastline of the East Cape, from the coastal town of Gisborne, round into the eastern Bay of Plenty.

At the southern end of Hawke Bay, another fine headland, Cape Kidnappers (so called by Cook when Maori attempted to kidnap some of his crew) is renowned for the large and approachable breeding colony of gannets (left). Cape Kidnappers is the only major mainland colony in New Zealand of the Australian gannet, a far-ranging sea bird which nests on the Cape through the summer months.

31

A seaside holiday has been part of the New Zealand way of life for generations. Some families have baches, owned by the family for as long as anyone living can remember, within a stones-throw of the sea. The bach at Papatea Bay (right) in the Bay of Plenty is typical of the homely baches, often built by the owners, to which New Zealand families made their annual escape from the city. Others prefer to pitch their tents at one of hundreds of seaside camping grounds around the coast, like the campground at Maungaroa (left, below), also in the Bay of Plenty, near Te Kaha.

Although there are baches at Hicks Bay (left, above), and families camp there in summer, away from the settlement and campground neither bach nor tent intrude on superb coastal scenery, typical of the scenery of long stretches of undeveloped coastline.

Many New Zealanders who holiday by the sea spend much of their time fishing. Castle Point (left) on the Wairarapa coast, is famous for its dramatic white headland and its lighthouse. Though lives have been lost when people have been swept off the curve of reef and islets which separates the lagoon from the open sea, it is a favoured place for surfcasting (right, above). The mouths of rivers are also good fishing spots. At Lake Ferry (right, below) on the southern Wairarapa coast, fishermen cast hopefully into waters where the rushing river contends with tides and swell.

At the north-eastern corner of the South Island, the sheltered waters of the Marlborough Sounds (right) contrast with the turbulent, often storm-wracked waters of Cook Strait, onto which the drowned valleys of the Sounds open. Two of the main sounds are Kenepuru (foreground) and Queen Charlotte (top right). Islands in Cook Strait, close to the entrances to the Sounds, are the only remaining refuges of a curious survivor, the tuatara (left), the single representative of an order of reptiles which otherwise became extinct one hundred million years ago.

West of the Marlborough Sounds, at the top of the South Island, Tasman and Golden Bays are separated by the bush-clad rocky headlands and golden-sand beaches of the Abel Tasman National Park (above), where sea-kayaking vies with walking as a holiday activity.

On the west coast of the South Island, nikau palms and tree ferns (left) give the shoreline an almost tropical feel, though the tropics are actually hundreds of kilometres to the north, and the Tasman Sea, which beats against the coast, is open to the Great Southern Ocean. Near Nelson, Tahunanui Beach (right), crowded on a summer day, is all but deserted when the dramatic light of a late winter afternoon sun breaks through the clouds. At the mouth of the Kahutara River (below, top) just south of Kaikoura, locals dip fine-meshed nets into the flowing water, hopeful of a catch of the delicacy whitebait. The Marlborough Sounds provide a sheltered passage for half the journey made by the Cook Strait ferries between Wellington and Picton. A ferry is seen here (below, bottom) leaving Picton.

At Punakaiki, on the South Island's west coast between Westport and Greymouth, an outcrop of stratified limestone has been eroded by a relentless sea into astonishing clefts and pillars, with layered walls and sides. The formation has been called, with descriptive accuracy, the Pancake Rocks (left). In a high sea, waves surge in clefts and spray spumes spectacularly from blowholes among the rocks. Near the Pancake Rocks themselves are more dramatic seascapes: gaunt sea stacks (above, top) and rocky headlands separating small sandy beaches (above, bottom).

The Kaikoura Coast (preceding pages), where high mountains plunge into a deep sea trench, has abundant marine life, from the fish which support a local fishing fleet to the whales and dolphins which draw nature tourists to the isolated town of Kaikoura.

Europeans have a matter-of-fact geological explanation for the formation of the round Moeraki Boulders (above) on the North Otago coast. They are concretions, eroded from softer formations by the sea. But to the Maori the boulders are gourds which were part of the cargo of the early Arai-te-uru canoe, which came to grief on nearby Shag Point.

The South Island's main city, Christchurch, is a few kilometres from the sea; its port, Lyttelton (right), is on the northern side of a long harbour which penetrates the northern side of Banks Peninsula. The harbour is, in truth, the eroded and flooded crater of a long-extinct volcano.

Far to the south, another great natural harbour, Paterson Inlet (following page) on Stewart Island could easily accommodate liners, container ships and tankers. Earlier this century there was a Norwegian whaling base on the north side of the Inlet, but today its broad waters are creased only by pleasure craft and fishing boats and around most of its long shoreline, bush still reaches down to the water's edge.

44

The southern coast of Southland looks across Foveaux Strait to Stewart Island, and beyond to the Great Southern Ocean. Ocean storms beat hard against the Southland coast, as windswept trees on Slope Point (this page, top) attest. Though cold, the waters of southern New Zealand teem with distinctive life, including the Dusky dolphin (this page, bottom), a denizen of Dusky Sound, and the endangered yellow-eyed penguin (this page, middle), which nests in small numbers at isolated rookeries around southern New Zealand.

At Te Waewae Bay (far left, opposite page) a quintessentially New Zealand contrast—between the settled farmland and tar-sealed road of civilisation in the foreground and the rugged mountains of the Fiordland wilderness beyond—give the landscape dramatic force.

The grandeur of wild New Zealand is nowhere seen in greater splendour than in the south-western corner of the South Island, where great fiords, gouged by glaciers then invaded by the sea, finger deep into a maze of steep, rugged, forest-clad mountains. Dusky Sound (following pages), explored by Captain Cook in 1773 on his second voyage to New Zealand, can be reached today only on foot or by boat or floatplane.

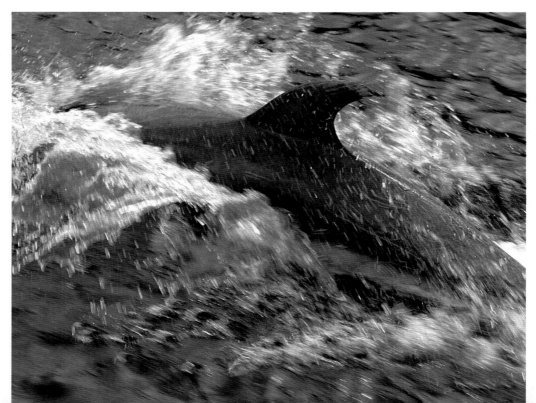

At the southern end of Fiordland, the mountains are lower and less dramatically steep. Though the scenery of Chalky and Preservation Inlets (the main picture, far left, is of sunrise at Chalky Inlet) is gentler than that of the sounds further north, it is still impressive. Doubtful Sound (left, above) is one of only two sounds accessible by road. The road over the Wilmot Pass was built when the Manapouri power scheme was under construction. The spectacular scenery of Milford Sound (left, below), accessible by road through the Homer Tunnel, also draws cruise ships in from the Tasman Sea.

In the unspoiled fastness of south-western Fiordland, the waters of Preservation Inlet are separated from virgin native forest by a narrow strand of rocky shore (left). At Southland's Te Waewae Bay (above) a clear stream ripples from its small lagoon into Foveaux Strait. Between the warm, frequented waters of Northland and these lonely southern inlets and bays, the long coastline of New Zealand (it matches in length the coastline of the forty-eight contiguous states of the United States) affords a variety of landscapes, habitats and recreational opportunities that few countries in the world can match.

CITIES & TOWNS

Always close to the sea or mountains

New Zealands relatively small population (of about 3.5 million) is concentrated in the countrys towns and cities. About eighty-five per cent of New Zealanders live in either the 'four main centres or the provincial cities. (Twenty-six per cent live in Auckland alone.) Because the pressure of the population on the land is light, the urban and natural worlds are still close in most parts of New Zealand. This is evident in New Zealands oldest European town, Russell (left), where the bush which clads the surrounding hills fingers into the town itself. Even in populous Auckland, Rangitoto Island and the Waitakere Ranges remind hurrying commuters or harassed shoppers that open space and even wilderness are never far away. The cities and towns of New Zealand have buildings of architectural interest and rich cultural lives, but what gives them their distinction are their settings. Three of the four main centres—Auckland, Wellington and Dunedin—have the open water of harbours in their midst. The fourth of the main centres, Christchurch, though built mostly on a flat plain, affords prospects from its streets of the tussock-covered slopes and rocky crags of the nearby Port Hills or of the more distant 'foothills' of the Southern Alps. (In most countries the 'foothills' would be considered, most decidedly, mountains.) New Zealand thus presents the paradox of a highly urbanised country in which wild open spaces are almost always visible and accessible.

The Bay of Islands is commonly regarded as the cradle of the modern New Zealand nation. Most of the earliest Europeans to come to New Zealand settled in this area which already supported a strong Maori population. At Waitangi, the dwelling of the British Resident, where a treaty was signed between several Maori chiefs and the British Crown on 6 February 1840, still stands on a low hill looking over the Bay. It is known today as the Treaty House (this page, below). Elsewhere in the Bay of Islands, at Kerikeri, New Zealand's oldest surviving stone building, the Stone Store (this page, top) was built between 1832 and 1836 as a storehouse for the mission station there. New Zealand's first capital, as a British colony, was on the Bay of Islands, but the country's first Governor soon moved the seat of his government south to the shores of the Waitemata Harbour, where the modern buildings of Auckland (right) now rise.

One of the most striking symbols of Auckland today is its Harbour Bridge (left), which vaults the waters of the Waitemata Harbour and allows commuters living on the North Shore a usually speedy journey to work in downtown Auckland. In evening, the lights of the downtown (this page, top) sparkle when seen from the summit of one of the volcanic cones which stud the isthmus between the Waitemata and Manukau Harbours across which Auckland has sprawled. For other Aucklanders, the Waitemata Harbour is not a barrier between home and work but an opportunity to pursue their favourite pastime, sailing. The marina and yachts of the picture (this page, above) demonstrate why Auckland has earned the nickname 'City of Sails'.

The Waikato River flows from the heart of the North Island to reach the Tasman Sea just south of Auckland. Hamilton (main picture, right), bisected by the lower Waikato, began life as a military settlement, founded immediately after the wars fought between the British and the Maori for possession of the rich lands of the Waikato, the source of Hamilton's wealth. Not far from Hamilton, another Waikato River town, Cambridge (above), has the pleasant appearance and unhurried pace of a hundred small New Zealand towns. Smaller again, the coastal town of Whitianga (this page, right) on the eastern side of the Coromandel Peninsula combines service of nearby farms with catering to holidaymakers from cities like Auckland and Hamilton.

The main port on the Bay of Plenty coast (principal exports are logs and paper from vast exotic forests inland) is Tauranga. Tauranga's 'suburb', Mount Maunganui (above) takes its name from a prominent geographical feature, the Mount itself (opposite page, left), which stands sentinel at the entrance to the Tauranga Harbour. Another major east coast port, Napier, on Hawke Bay, has become renowned in recent years for its Art Deco architecture. On the Napier foreshore is a charming statue of Pania of the Reef (this page, left). A local legend tells of Pania, a sea maiden, forsaking the sea to marry a chief, then being turned into an off-shore reef because the gods of the sea were angry about her divided loyalties when she swam out from shore again.

Most New Zealanders live near the coast, but several larger secondary towns and cities are some distance from the sea. Rotorua, inland from the Bay of Plenty, first developed as a centre for tourists visiting its 'thermal wonderland'. The former Government Bath-house (left), set in fine gardens, now houses a museum and art gallery. It was built when it was hoped Rotorua would become a thermal spa. Masterton (above), the main town of the rural Wairarapa, exists to service the surrounding farms. Palmerston North, on the other side of the Tararua Range from Masterton, with its expansive central square (right) is also primarily an agricultural service town.

The downtown of New Zealand's capital city, Wellington, hugs the shores of a superb harbour, Port Nicholson (right). Toi toi (a New Zealand relative of South America's pampas grass) and pohutukawa flourish in the Town Belt which surrounds the inner city. Many of Wellington's houses cling to the steep slopes of the hills around the harbour or shelter in the gullies below the hills. The older wooden houses of the inner suburb of Thorndon (this page, top) had become run-down before the suburb again became a fashionable place to live. The main focus of Wellington, and of the whole country's political life, are Parliament Buildings (this page, above). A never-completed Parliament House of the early 1920s stands beside the Beehive (officially known as the Executive Wing) which was opened by the Queen in 1977 but not occupied until 1980. The concept for its design was suggested by Sir Basil Spence, an eminent English architect.

At the heart of Christchurch, the South Island's largest city, stands a noble Gothic church, the Anglican Cathedral (opposite page) built in several stages in the second half of the nineteenth century and today the city's undisputed symbol. A nineteenth century statue of the 'founder of Canterbury', John Robert Godley, contemplates the Cathedral from the centre of Cathedral Square.

Most of Christchurch is built on flat land, a corner of the extensive Canterbury Plains; from the hill suburbs on the southern side of the city, the distant ranges of the Southern Alps rise on the far side of the Plains (this page, top). Flowing through the heart of Christchurch, the Avon River (this page, middle) contributes, by its name and its appearance, to the English atmosphere which many profess to find in Christchurch. Central Christchurch turned the loss of its university to a suburban site to its advantage, by creating an Arts Centre out of the university's old grey-stone Gothic buildings, and building a lively Worcester Boulevard (this page, bottom) to link the Cathedral and the Canterbury Museum past the Arts Centre.

The port town of the southern city of Dunedin, Port Chalmers (right) sits half-way up the Otago Harbour, where the water is still deep enough for ocean-going vessels. South of Dunedin, the small country town of Balclutha (above, top) sits in the flood-prone crook of a meander of the lower Clutha River, New Zealand's largest (though not longest) river. In North Otago, the coastal town on Oamaru (above, lower) built itself an artificial port in the nineteenth century, but the port is now used only by pleasure craft and Oamaru, like many secondary towns and cities in New Zealand, struggles to maintain its size and economic vitality.

Briefly in the nineteenth century, when the lure of gold brought miners in their thousands to Otago, Dunedin was New Zealand's largest and most prosperous city. The Scottish Presbyterian founders of the Otago Settlement (founded before gold was discovered in the hinterland) laid Dunedin out with a distinctive Octagon at its centre (left). The Scottish respect for education contributed to the founding of New Zealand's first university in Dunedin in 1869, a year before the University of New Zealand was established by an Act of Parliament. Otago University's original, dignified, grey-stone buildings (above) still stand at the heart of the large modern institution that Otago University has become. Dunedin is notable for other fine buildings of the Victorian and Edwardian years of its prime, including the fine Railway Station and solid Court Buildings (right).

New Zealand's most southerly city, Invercargill (above), was established in the 1850s, when the first settlers began living on the 'mere bog ... unfit for habitation' (as an early surveyor described the site) on the southern edge of the fertile and well-watered Southland Plain, close to the broad New River estuary. Southland's other main town, Gore (opposite page, bottom) sits in the valley of the Mataura River. A distant view from the downs that surround the town shows how open to, and dependent on, the surrounding farmland are most of New Zealand's country towns. North of Invercargill, where Southland merges into Central Otago, sinuous Lake Wakatipu occupies a superb mountain setting. Queenstown (opposite page, top) nestles round a bay on the lake's shore and is overlooked by the striking Remarkable Mountains. Beginning life as a gold-mining town, Queenstown has prospered in recent years as a tourist destination.

F A R M L A N D S

Fertile valleys, plains & foothills

Although New Zealand enjoys an international reputation as a natural, unspoiled place, human beings have wrought profound and enormous changes on its landscapes and habitats. These changes began with the arrival of the Polynesian ancestors of the Maori. Their fires reduced the country's area of forest, notably in the drier regions on the eastern sides of each of the main islands. But it was only with the arrival of Europeans in the nineteenth century that a full-scale onslaught on New Zealand's natural mantle of forest began. The settlers' fires and axes turned large areas of New Zealand into pasture, like the South Canterbury downlands near Fairlie (left) which in times long past were forested. These pasture lands now support the livestock, like the sheep safely grazing, on which New Zealand's prosperity still to a large extent depends. The grasses, clover and other plants of these pastures are almost all introduced (mostly from Europe) and over much of rural New Zealand indigenous trees are far less common than exotics—pines, macrocarpas, willows and poplars. But for all this transformation of much New Zealand into farmland, an older New Zealand is still present. What gives many of the country's rural landscapes their appeal is the juxtaposition of neatly ordered farmland with native bush and wild ranges. The landscapes over much of New Zealand have been transformed in the past 150 years, but reminders of wild and undeveloped land still intrude. The foreground detail may be ordered, even English, but the over-all scene is often a combination of the 'wild and won' (as a New Zealand poet put it) which is distinctively New Zealand's.

ost of lowland New Zealand has been turned from forest into farmland. Although crops are grown in great variety, New Zealand is a pastoral rather than agricultural country. Near Karitane, just north of Dunedin, winter sun burns the frost off pasture (right, opposite page). Near Geraldine, some of New Zealand's millions of sheep graze on introduced pastures (above), beneath pylons that carry electricity from the hydro stations of the Waitaki Valley to power-hungry cities further north. Most of rural New Zealand is now divided into small farms, owned and run by single families. But in the nineteenth century, large areas of parts of the country were swallowed up in vast estates running huge flocks of sheep which were shorn in big woolsheds, like the stone 'shed' at Morven Hills, near Omarama in inland Otago (right, this page).

M*uch of the diversification in New Zealand farming of the past thirty years, away from pure pastoralism, has occurred in places with favourable climates, like the sheltered, north-facing valleys of Nelson. Near Motupiko (opposite page), south-west of Nelson city, mist lingers in warm, well-watered and fertile valleys. In the past two or three decades, diversification has been the catch-cry of many New Zealand farmers. Experiments with different crops in different parts of the country have given New Zealand a broader base of farm exports and the New Zealand consumer a wider range of home grown products to choose from. These have included sunflowers, for seed and oil, (this page, top left); grapes, for the fast-growing and successful wine industry, (this page, left middle); apples, which have become a major export item, (this page, left bottom); apricots, grown in near ideal conditions in Central Otago where harsh winters are followed by hot summers, (this page, top right); tulips, which are air-freighted to markets as far away as Asia and Europe, (this page, right middle); and kiwi fruit, a fruit developed in New Zealand, which gave some growers boom years in the 1970s and 1980s, (this page, right bottom).*

There are more sheep than any other farm animal in New Zealand and though sheep numbers fluctuate according to the seasons and overseas prices for wool and meat, sheep usually outnumber people by about twenty to one. Although New Zealand no longer enjoys a secure market for almost all the wool and meat it produces in Great Britain, and New Zealand as a whole has diversified its exports remarkably in the past thirty years, those two commodities still earn the country a significant proportion of its export earnings. Favoured breeds of sheep produce both wool and meat, like the ewes and their half-grown lambs in the yards of a large North Canterbury property, Leslie Hills (left). A country which has depended as heavily as New Zealand has on farm exports has accumulated an interesting heritage of farm buildings, from the great woolsheds like Morven Hills (page 82) to a humble farm shed (below) at Tahakopa, in the Catlins region of Southland, built of poles of a native wood, kowhai, and rough planks.

*S*heep predominate in the drier parts of New Zealand, but where the rainfall is higher and more reliable, lush pastures support dairy herds. Moist Taranaki (the province took its name from the mountain which dominates it) is one of the country's main dairying regions (opposite page). Horse-racing is popular in New Zealand and New Zealand-bred racehorses command high prices from overseas buyers at New Zealand sales. The Blandford Lodge Stud at Matamata in the Waikato (above) is typical of the many stud farms to be found on both islands. Hill country as well as flat land is regularly cultivated in New Zealand, sometimes to put down in crops, sometimes as a first step in establishing high quality pasture. In the hill country south of Te Kuiti (this page, left) a local farmer is ploughing part of his holding.

The Canterbury Plains, and the downlands fringing its inland edges, are one of New Zealand's major cropping areas and the only area where significant quantities of cereals are grown. From the air, the mosaic when closely subdivided land is used to grow various crops is apparent on the Canterbury Plains near Darfield (right, opposite page), west of Christchurch. In late summer and early autumn, header harvesters reaping and threshing 'fields of golden grain' in a single pass are a familiar sight on South Canterbury downs (above). New Zealand farming is highly mechanised. Today's farmers use a farmbike, rather than horse or foot, to get around their properties or work their stock (right, this page).

New Zealand farmland often has a drama and strength lacking in the rural landscapes of longer occupied, more closely settled countries. Bright sunlight glances brilliantly over typical sheep country (left) near Fairlie in South Canterbury. Many New Zealand landscapes seem often rather empty to visitors from older settled countries. But the usual clutter of buildings and signs is certainly present in the New Zealand countryside: a whata or storehouse on a farm at Peria (right, top); a sign advertising kumara, an important crop in the Dargaville area of Northland (right, middle); shearers' quarters at the Shag Valley Station, Otago (right, bottom); a bach at Lake Tekapo, South Canterbury (far right, top); a sign boasting the town's production of sausages, Tuatapere, Southland (far right, middle); a farm building at Taihape, in the central North Island (far right, bottom).

Wild deer were once a serious pest, destroying native forests and other plant communities that played a role in reducing erosion. Now domesticated and earning New Zealand valuable funds from exports of venison and velvet, the creatures once hunted through wild mountains now graze fertile river flats in pampered comfort. A deer farm at Paradise, near the head of Lake Wakatipu, (preceding pages) is in sight of country where deer once roamed wild. Beyond the farm rear dramatic ranges which run back into the mountain wilderness of the Mount Aspiring National Park.

Some of New Zealand's most appealing landscapes are where clear, cultivated land lies close to country where the native vegetation— bush, scrub or tussock grassland—still predominates. On the Kenepuru Sound, in Marlborough, still forested hills contrast cleanly with green pasture (right). Although the scene lacks bush, something of the same 'feel' is evident near Burkes Pass, South Canterbury, (above), where land cultivated for crops merges directly into tussock grassland which continues on into wild, more distant hills.

Landscapes in which settled farmland contrasts with still untamed country are to be found throughout New Zealand, from Tapapa, where the Kaimai Ranges provide a contrasting backdrop for a neat farm (left, opposite page), to the Wanganui River valley, where rugged, bush-clad hills seem to hem in cleared hill pasture and fields by the river (above), to the Arrow Basin, in Central Otago, where stern, rocky ranges overlook farmland on the floor of the basin (left, this page).

In their eagerness to create pasture, the European pioneers cleared even steep, rugged hill country of its native cover of forest. The once-forested hills of the Whareama district of the Wairarapa (above, left) are now clear grassland, with farm tracks and artificial water holes for stock indicating the uses to which the land is now put, and the occasional slip hinting that some of the land at least, in country so steep, should have been left in bush. Banks Peninsula, south of Christchurch, was also largely forested when the European pioneers arrived, but is now mostly open hill pasture, as in this view looking down the length of the Akaroa Harbour (left). Further south on the South Island's east coast, Otago Peninsula has also been cleared and turned into pasture. In the foreground of this view of the Otago Peninsula (above, right) is Larnach Castle, the Scottish Baronial home of a nineteenth century politician, banker and merchant.

Rural New Zealand has generally a casual, unhurried air about it. Few motorists become impatient when journeys are slowed by mobs of sheep or cattle being driven along country roads. In the picture, a large flock of sheep is being urged gently along a road at Glenaray, Southland (above). Farming in New Zealand is easier because the country has an equable climate—stock graze outside all year round and when snow does fall on the lowlands, as here in South Canter-

bury (right), it seldom lies for more than a few days.

In wetter and rougher country, New Zealand farmers generally run cattle rather than sheep. On the cleared river flats of the Fox River in South Westland (following pages), against a superb background of the highest peaks of the Southern Alps, a mixed herd of Hereford and Aberdeen Angus cattle graze the rough, lank pastures of this high-rainfall area.

Though the mountains of North Westland are lower than those of South Westland, near Charleston, the Paparoa Range still provides a dramatic backdrop for pockets of farmed land, cleared from the scrub and bush (this page, lower). From the air, the typical patterns of New Zealand farmland are readily apparent. On the easier country, there are closely subdivided paddocks; the country roads are often metalled rather than tar-sealed; and exotic trees planted in clumps or belts provide shelter for stock and protect the soil from erosion by the winds which result from New Zealand's mid-ocean location. A similar pattern is evident from one end of the country to the other—from farmland in Southland, north-east of Gore (right), to a horse stud near Cambridge in the Waikato (this page, top), hundreds of kilometres north, across Cook Strait.

WILD NEW ZEALAND

Mountains, lakes, rivers, forests & geothermal activity

New Zealand has an excellent system of sealed main roads. But it is often the case, in this lightly populated country, that not too far off the main highways, the side roads peter out and the visitor enters an unspoiled New Zealand of dense bush (as New Zealanders still commonly call their native forests) and crystal-clear streams, bordered and overhung with ferns (left). Many of these streams begin with melt water from snowfields high on the country's many mountain ranges and feed into turbulent rivers which fall swiftly to the sea. Much of this relatively unchanged wild country of New Zealand is protected as national park, reserve or forest park. New Zealand has no fewer than twelve national parks, the borders of which encompass two million hectares. Another three million hectares are protected as forest park or reserve. Nearly one-fifth of the country's total land area is under some form of protection for conservation purposes. The largest of New Zealand's national parks, Fiordland, occupies the south-western corner of the South Island, an area of such scenic magnificence, so little marred by the impact of human beings, that it has been given World Heritage status. In my childhood, maps of Fiordland still bore the word 'unexplored' over certain areas and in the late 1940s, a bird thought long extinct, the takahe, was rediscovered alive in a remote Fiordland valley. In New Zealand's wild places are many lakes, large and small. The largest of them all, the central North Island's Lake Taupo, occupies a depression left by a cataclysmic volcanic explosion. But the South Island's southern lakes, from Tekapo to Manapouri, mostly of glacial origin, surpass Taupo in splendour if not in size. Wild New Zealand is a land of rugged mountains, calm lakes, and turbulent rivers, a land that is sometimes dangerous and frightening, but a land also which rewards those who visit it with splendour and beauty.

Two thousand years ago, almost 80 per cent of New Zealand was forest-covered. Today only 20 per cent of the land is forested, and most of that is steeper country. Of some lowland forest communities only isolated fragments remain. But there are still extensive tracts of forest in hilly or mountainous country. Northland's Man-gamuka River (above) flows clear from bush-clad hills, past the giant tree ferns that give much of New Zealand's bush an exotic, even primeval, character. Much of Northland and the Coromandel were covered, when Europeans reached New Zealand, with majestic kauri forest. Highly prized for their timber, only a few kauri survive in reserves. The survivors include such giants as Te Matua Ngahere the Lord of the Forest, (right, opposite page). On unspoiled lake margins and swamp edges, the grace-ful toi toi still flutters in the wind (right).

A rugged country, lifted high out of the sea by the massive forces of colliding tectonic plates, New Zealand has an abundance of waterfalls. They include Fiordland's high Sutherland Falls (the highest in the country) and the mighty Huka Falls in the central North Island, where the entire Waikato River is forced through a narrow defile. But perhaps more typical of the country's waterfalls are the graceful Bridal Veil Falls near Raglan (left), where a small bush stream tumbles over a limestone escarpment. New Zealand is also well-endowed with natural lakes, large and small. The development of the country's hydro-electric resources has added to their number. Lake Karapiro (above) was formed when the Waikato River was dammed not far south of Hamilton in 1947. This was the first major hydro station built on the Waikato River after World War II. Lake Karapiro is now only one of several artificial lakes on New Zealand's longest river.

New Zealand sits astride the boundary between two tectonic plates. Vulcanism is a feature of such plate boundaries. New Zealand is at the western end of the Pacific's 'rim of fire'. Volcanic rocks occur throughout the country, but volcanoes active to this day are found only on the North Island or, in the case of White Island (above), just off its coast. White Island, the most fiercely active of all New Zealand's volcanoes, can be seen steaming and smoking from the Bay of Plenty coast. Today Mount Tarawera slumbers peacefully on the far side of the placid lake of the same name (right). It does not even look particularly like a volcano. But its summit is rent by a spectacular gash and in 1886, Tarawera erupted with dramatic force, devastating a huge area of the central North Island.

M*any of the magnificent old trees of New Zealand's virgin forest are hundreds of years old. To many New Zealanders, Pakeha as well as Maori, such trees possess spiritual power. The fissured trunk of an ancient rata (left, opposite page) in the Urewera National Park, hints at such power. Centre piece of the Urewera National Park is bush-girt Lake Waikaremoana, from whose* *'rippling waters' the Panekiri Bluff rears up impressively (above). Many of New Zealand's forests are regarded by botanists as temperate rain forests; they are sustained by the abundant rain which falls in many parts of the country. This same abundant rainfall causes mosses and ferns to flourish on shaded cliff faces and banks (left, this page).*

In the very centre of the North Island, three active volcanoes rise out of the vast volcanic plateau (above). Ruapehu, left, is the highest of these volcanoes and Ngauruhoe, right, the most active. Lake Taupo, in the foreground, is itself of volcanic origin. The last of the great pumice eruptions from Taupo occurred as recently as 1800 years ago. Water subsequently filled the area of subsidence to form today's lake.

Many North Island waterfalls are still found in attractive bush settings. In the ranges surrounding Lake Waikaremoana, the falls called Te Tangi Te Hinerau, the tears of Hinerau, (right) cascade over a rocky ledge in such a setting.

On the summit of the North Island's highest mountain, the volcano Ruapehu, a hot crater lake (left) steams eerily amid the snow and ice surrounding it. In 1954, a sudden breaching of the crater wall sent a lahar, a surge of water and mud, down the Whangaehu River. At Tangiwai, the lahar swept away a railway bridge and caused New Zealand's worst rail disaster when a crowded express train plunged from the broken bridge into the swollen river. On the bleak, wind-swept, rocky slopes of the volcanoes of the central North Island, tenacious alpine plants (below) cling to crevices or root in small pockets of soil. Many of these plants are related to, but different from, the alpine plants of the South Island's Southern Alps.

ount Ngauruhoe
(right, opposite page) is the youngest and most active
of the central North Island's trio of active volcanoes.
Sacred to the Tuwharetoa tribe, which occupied the
land around the mountains, the peaks were given to
the people of New Zealand in 1887 by the chief of the
tribe, Te Heuheu Tukino, on condition they were
protected from exploitation or abuse. In 1894, legis-
lation created the Tongariro National Park, New
Zealand's first.

Evidence of geothermal activity is also striking,
elsewhere in the central North Island, at Rotorua,
which has drawn tourists for more than a hundred
years to view its boiling mud pools (right, this page)
and geysers, the grandest of which is Pohutu (above)
at Whakarewarewa.

Hot springs, steaming earth, boiling lakes and mineral deposits make the Rotorua and other geothermal areas seem eerie, even sinister, places to some visitors. In the Waiotapu thermal valley, just south of Rotorua, hot water lakes, occupying craters formed by steam explosions, sit on the flank of Rainbow Mountain. In certain places within the North Island's geothermal regions, the abundant natural steam has been harnessed to generate electric power, a technology in which New Zealand has a world ranking.

From the slopes of Mount Ruapehu, the fine, near symmetrical, cone of Taranaki (Mount Egmont) can be seen across the intervening hill country (below). Maori legend tells of Taranaki once occupying a position in the centre of the Island, beside Ruapehu, Tongariro and Ngauruhoe. Rivalry between Taranaki and Tongariro for the love of Ruapehu resulted in a titanic battle. Taranaki was defeated and fled west, carving out the course of Whanganui River and finally coming to rest many kilometres to the west, on the far edge of the North Island. One of the tributaries of the Whanganui River which Taranaki carved out on his flight westwards is the Mangawhero. Not far from its confluence with the Whanganui, the Mangawhero cascades over the impressive Raukawa Falls (right), framed by a fragment of the bush which once covered all the surrounding hills, most of them now cleared and in pasture.

The mountain ranges of the South Island run from one end of the Island to the other. The high snowy summits, broad glacier-carved valleys, vast inter-montane basins and great lakes of this broad, complex belt of ranges give New Zealand some of its grandest scenery. Most northerly of the large mountain lakes of the Southern Alps are the Nelson Lakes, sources of the mighty Buller River, which forces its way through stern gorges to the Tasman Sea. On a calm evening on Lake Rotoiti (left), the bush-clad Travers and St Arnaud Ranges can be seen embracing the head of the lake. In the valley of the Wairau River, which rises close to Lake Rotoiti but flows east to the Pacific Ocean rather than west to the Tasman Sea, native beech forest (above), typical of the drier eastern ranges of the South Island, flanks the valley's sides. Though this forest is less damp than the western rain forests, mosses flourish in its cool shade.

The South Island's mountain ranges afford abundant and varied opportunities for recreation. Trampers, shooters, mountain climbers and skiers all take advantage of the Southern Alps (the term is sometimes used to refer to just the highest mountains of the Central Alps, sometimes to refer to all the ranges down the spine of the Island). Trampers in the Edwards Valley in the Arthur's Pass National Park (above, left) pause for a drink from the clear water of the river. An easy days walk from the road has taken them into unspoiled mountain country. The mountain climate can,

however, be harsh and a stark contrast with the summer sun in the Edwards Valley is provided by snow and hoar frost on trees at Burkes Pass (above, right).

Most of the South Island's ranges are made up of a brittle sedimentary rock called greywacke. A few of the ranges are composed of other rocks, including schists, granites and the 'marble' (actually an altered limestone) of North-west Nelson. On Nelson's Takaka Hill, this marble has weathered into intriguing surface forms (left).

A *number of named tracks provide trips of several days duration through spectacular areas of the South Island's mountains. The most famous of these is Fiordland's Milford Track. Further north, where North Canterbury and southern Nelson merge in a complex knot of mountains, the St James Walkway takes hikers through the scenic Ada Valley (above).*

The rivers of the eastern South Island owe their power and the volume of water they carry to the high rainfall in their mountain catchments. Issuing onto the Canterbury Plains, these rivers, like the Waimakariri (right), sprawl in braided channels over open shingle beds. Some of the water they carry from the mountains to the sea is used on the dry plains to water stock and for irrigation. The straight line to the right of the river is a channel carrying water taken from the river for these purposes.

The air of the South Island's Mackenzie Country, in the dry lee of the Central Alps is crisply clear. That clarity of air at Lake Tekapo allowed the progress of a lunar eclipse over the lake to be captured on film (below). Even when cloud and mist mask the Mackenzie Country's skies, the light is still exceptional, as when sunlight and shadow scud over the Richmond Range near Lake Tekapo (this page, left) or a rainbow arches down onto the lake's surface (opposite page).

As a cold, steely dawn breaks over the tangled ranges of the Central Alps (following pages), low cloud, like cotton wool, fingers up the deep, gorged valleys of Westland towards Mount Elie de Beaumont, the most northerly of the highest mountains of the Alps.

T he barrier of the Southern Alps forces moisture-laden westerly winds blowing in from the Tasman Sea high into a cold atmosphere. The precipitation that results—the heaviest snow and rain falls in the country—swells tempestuous rivers, fills numerous lakes, and nourishes dense rain forests, in which ferns and mosses compete fiercely in the dense undergrowth (right). In the lowland section of the Westland National Park, Lake Mapourika (this page, top) lies in a hollow of the huge moraines deposited by the much larger glaciers of earlier 'ice ages'. Further south, State Highway 6 skirts Lake Moeraki (this page, lower) in its bush-clad valley.

The same winds which bring prodigious amounts of rain and snow to the western side of the Southern Alps blow hot and dry in the 'rain shadow' areas east of the Main Divide. Instead of lush green bush are the dry tussock range lands of areas like the Lindis Pass (following page). Often only a few kilometres, but also high mountains, separate the forests of Westland from the dry grasslands of inland Canterbury and Otago.

1 In South Westland, the Southern Alps rear up abruptly from a narrow coastal plain. The high neves which feed the great glaciers of the region are visible from wild beaches. From Lake Matheson (right) near Fox Glacier, New Zealand's highest peaks loom more than 3,000 metres through the morning mist, Tasman to the left and Cook to the right. Parts of the South Westland plain and lowlands have been cleared for farming. The spectacular background for this farm shed near the Fox Glacier township (below) is the snowfields and part of the trunk of the Fox Glacier.

Rare denizen of the South Island's mountain forests is the native robin (left). When seen the robin will often watch people curiously, leading an early New Zealand poet to write of 'the daring robin, all unused to wrong'.

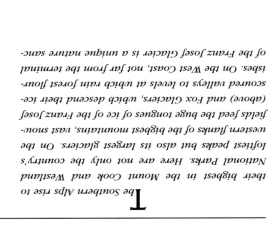

T he Southern Alps rise to their highest in the Mount Cook and Westland National Parks. Here are not only the country's loftiest peaks but also its largest glaciers. On the western flanks of the highest mountains, vast snow-fields feed the huge tongues of ice of the Franz Josef (above) and Fox Glaciers, which descend their ice-scoured valleys to levels at which rain forest flour-ishes. On the West Coast, not far from the terminal of the Franz Josef Glacier is a unique nature sanc-

tuary on the Okarito Lagoon—the only place in the country where the rare kotuku or white heron nests (opposite page). Also unique to the New Zealand mountains is the kea—the world's only parrot truly adapted to an alpine environment. Intelligent, curious and mischievous, kea are favourites of people who frequent the mountains. In flight, the vivid red of the under-wings is visible, and the stories of their pranks and antics are legion.

New Zealand's two highest peaks bear the names of the European mariners who 'discovered' then 'rediscovered' New Zealand in the seventeenth and eighteenth centuries—Tasman and Cook. But the highest peak, Cook, is also commonly, and increasingly, referred to as Aoraki, the traditional name by which the South Island's Ngai Tahu, last of the tribes which occupied the Island for hundreds of years before the arrival of Europeans, knew the mountain. Aoraki/ Mount Cook (above) lies between the Tasman, in the right distance, and Hooker, in the left foreground,

Glaciers. These are two of the great rivers of ice that flow from the flanks of the highest mountains. Cook and Tasman look distant when seen across the expanse of the Fox Neve (far left), the massive accumulation of snow and ice brought by westerly winds to the mountains. The 'Main Divide' is a formidable barrier between the wetter west and drier east of the South Island. Cook, left, and Tasman, right, terminate this view (left) looking south along the crest of this barrier from above Grahams Saddle, one of the few points at which mountaineers can cross the barrier with relative ease.

Below the forbidding mountains of the Alps lie gentler plains and attractive lakes. A dusty road beside Lake Ohau (far right, opposite page) leads towards the valley of one of the rivers which flow from the snowfields and glaciers of the mountains.

The abrupt transition from ice-bound heights to warm, fertile lowlands gives New Zealand a flora of great variety and astonishing, though often hidden or subtle, beauty. The gold of kowhai (this page, left top) is so loved by many New Zealanders it has become a national emblem. Lichens (this page, left middle) flourish from the highest rocks on Mount Cook to the coast. The misnamed Mount Cook lily (this page, left bottom), really a giant buttercup, is the grandest of New Zealand's alpine flowers. Mountain daisies (this page, right top) occur in great variety, from these large blooms to tiny mat plants. The New Zealand mistletoe (this page, right middle) provides dramatic splashes of red in sombre green bush. The copious rainfall of many parts of New Zealand means the country has an abundance of mosses and ferns (this page, right bottom) among its native plants.

The South Island's high country, the dry, tussock-clad ranges and basins east of the Southern Alps, have undergone disturbing ecological changes since Europeans first began to run sheep there. But it has remained an area of magnificent prospects and of a profound, still loneliness, never more so than when the last light of day brushes the snowfields of distant mountains, as at Lake Tekapo (left, opposite page), or the sides of Mounts Cook and Tasman (left, this page), towering at the head of the Tasman Valley. Since the first Europeans took up land in the high country, it has been used for running sheep. By Lake Tekapo, grateful runholders erected a memorial to the companion that made it possible to manage huge flocks of sheep on the vast grasslands of the Mackenzie Plain, the sheep dog (above).

When Europeans first entered the high country, it was a harsh, open and windswept land. But over more than a century, corners of this raw country have been tamed. By Lake Middleton (above), tiny companion of larger Lake Ohau, exotic trees and wildflowers create a sheltered and domesticated foreground which contrasts with the bare wild ranges beyond. In the Lindis Pass, poplars, just on autumn's turn, guard the evocative ruins of an old hotel (left, this page), where drovers and waggon drivers, in the days when travel was slower, found welcome rest for the night. But in most parts of the high country, the imprint of human occupation is scarcely evident and it remains a land of solitude and open spaces. By the swift, clear Ahuriri River (left, opposite page), erosion has sculpted low cliffs into fantastic pinnacles and battlements.

157

*A*lthough the Arrow Basin (right), near Queenstown, at the southern end of the South Island's high country, is relatively closely settled and in places even intensively farmed, it retains the sense of wide open space and the predominantly fawn and yellow colouration of the more remote parts of the high country. The Kawarau River, fringed with introduced willows, drains the best-known of the Southern Lakes, Wakatipu, on which Queenstown stands. Not far from the lake's outlet, a jet boat (developed originally for use on the South Islands swift shallow rivers) makes an exciting dash between the rocks that stud the river's channel. The Remarkable Range, also visible from Queens-town, provides a spectacular background for the excitement of riding the swift river.

Some of the most exciting jet boat and raft rides in all of New Zealand are made on the Shotover River which, not far from Queenstown, flows through the dramatic Skippers Canyon (left). From the Canyon, working often in appalling conditions through hard winters, early miners took impressive amounts of alluvial gold. The road from Queenstown to the Shotover and the old goldmining town of Arrowtown passes through country boldly shaped by the ice of ancient glaciers (right above). The sometimes harsh landscapes of the district are now softened by exotic trees, which flare golden in autumn, reminding many travellers of the real gold which brought hardy miners to the district in the 1860s. The same gold of autumn frames the wind-ruffled waters of picturesque Lake Hayes (right, below) which is also not far from Queenstown.

Lake Wakatipu twists for nearly eighty kilometres through the rugged mountains of western Otago. At the head of Wakatipu, the Humboldt, Ailsa and Forbes Mountains rise dramatically beyond the lake. On some of the most remote stations in New Zealand, reached only by rough gravel roads or by boat across the lake, cattle and sheep graze the narrow riverbed or lakeside flats. At Mount Creighton Station (right) the colours that make autumn one of the favoured times to visit the region contrast with sombre evergreens and the dark brooding mountains beyond. The great Southern Lakes are all accessible by road, but high in the mountains are countless smaller lakes or tarns that can only be seen from the air or reached on foot. High above the tree line, the cold, rock-bound waters of Lake Castalia (above), above the Wilkin Valley beyond the head of Lake Wanaka, are fed by snow melting from the mountains that encircle the lake.

One of the tributaries of the Makarora River, which flows into the head of Lake Wanaka, is the Wilkin, which rises in the wilderness ranges of the Mount Aspiring National Park. People who tramp up the Wilkin (the valley, like hundreds in the Southern Alps, has no road) are rewarded by a view of noble Mount Pollux (right) framed by a characteristically glacier-shaped valley. The lower slopes of the steep valley wall are forested, but above the bush line and the narrow belt of subalpine scrub and grassland are bare rock and permanent snowfields. Further east, away from the high rainfall of the mountains, the only trees on the slopes above Lake Wanaka (above) are introduced willows and pines. But beside Lake Hawea (left) the native cabbage tree (surprisingly a member of the lily family) provide an indigenous foreground for a superb view of the Sentinel and Terrace Peaks.

The south-western corner of the South Island is occupied by New Zealand's largest national park, Fiordland. The Park takes its name from the deep fiords or sounds, carved by ancient glaciers and flooded by the sea, which penetrate into some of the ruggedest ranges in all New Zealand. On the eastern edge of Fiordland, two of New Zealand's most beautiful lakes, Te Anau and Manapouri, lap against the inland edge of these ranges. The Doubtful Islands (right) lie at the entrance to Lake Te Anau's Middle Fiord. Though wild and rugged, Fiordland has gentle, peaceful valleys. Some of the loveliest of these valleys are now accessible by road. A road was built up the Grebe Valley (above, top), which flows into Lake Manapouri, so a transmission line from the Manapouri power scheme could be constructed. The Mirror Lakes (above, lower) are close to the highway to Milford Sound, in the Eglinton Valley.

On the gentler eastern
shore of Lake Te Anau, near the southern end of the
lake, is the small township of Te Anau. On the
summer-placid lake, just off the town, are moored
the boats (above) which are used to explore the
lake's myriad bush-fringed bays, inlets and islets.
Tracks and huts, like the hut (right) in the Caples
Valley, have opened many of the valleys in Fiordland
which lack roads for superb tramping and hiking.

The Caples Valley is on Fiordland's eastern fringe, where the head of Lake Wakatipu and Milford Sound, though a long journey apart by road, are surprisingly close. Mount Talbot (right), at the head of the Hollyford Valley, provides one of the more magnificent views from the road into Milford Sound, which was opened in 1953, after completion of the Homer Tunnel.

One of the more popular walking tracks in Fiordland is the Routeburn which crosses the Humboldt Mountains, past Lake Harris, from the head of Lake Wakatipu to the Milford Road. In summer, the track passes through sun-dappled beech forest and over golden snowgrass. But part of the route of the track is seen here (left) when the mountains are mantled in winter's snow and Lake Harris is frozen. Just how lovely Fiordland, forbidding in winter, can be in summer is evident with the sun shining through beech forest on the shore of Lake McKellar (this page, top), near the western end of the Routeburn Track. Equally, that much of Fiordland is rugged and wild, and no place for the inexperienced or ill-equipped, is obvious from the air, looking down on Nor'-west Lake (this page, lower), cradled in a high valley above distant Lake Manapouri.

The scenic gem of Fiordland—perhaps of the whole of New Zealand— is the view of Mitre Peak across the waters, sometimes calm, at others rough, of Milford Sound (right, opposite page). The grandeur of sheer rock walls plummeting to mysterious depths is not surpassed in many places on the Earth's surface. The building of the Milford Road (excavation of the Homer Tunnel began in 1935 and the mountain was pierced by 1940, but the war delayed completion of the road until 1953) made this spectacular view readily accessible. From the boat harbour at the road's end on the edge of Milford Sound (above), with low mist obscuring parts of the view up the Arthur Valley, the Sound has an air of mystery and grandeur.

But the appeal of New Zealand is not just in vast and magnificent landscapes. It is found, too in the detail of an extraordinarily rich and diverse native vegetation, in which ferns (right, this page) occupy an important place. Unique native plants have survived the impact of one thousand years of human occupation, especially in the mountains and wilderness that still occupy large areas of 'these islands in the Pacific sun'. A 'sense of noiseless sweet escape', rare now in many countries but still an accessible experience in New Zealand's wilderness areas and mountains and along its superb and lonely coasts, is, by most New Zealanders, simply taken for granted.